THE · OF · TANTALON · TASKS

A Fantasy Questbook

Do you have the wisdom, wit and courage to complete Tantalon's great adventure quest?

Devised and written by
Steve Jackson

illustrated by
Stephen Lavis

Puffin Books
in association with Oxford University Press

THE TASKS OF TANTALON

THE War of the Four Kingdoms was over! Tantalon replaced his quill. The Treaty of Peace had been negotiated, agreed and was now sealed in writing. The four nobles rose to their feet. A fanfare sounded as the others turned away from the ageing wizard and walked towards the door. Slowly and deliberately Tantalon lowered himself into his seat and sighed....

The war had been long and bloody, a senseless waste of life. The death toll had even taken Gallantaria's own King Constain and his Queen, ambushed and butchered by Northlanders in Narrow Pass. This tragedy had dealt a severe blow to the Kingdom of Gallantaria. The King had left no heirs. Who was to rule?

An emergency meeting of the Knights of the Inner Council was called. There was much vying for power as the knights argued. For two days and nights the debate continued fruitlessly. Finally it was the bearded Sir Duke who suggested that the Crown be held by Tantalon, Sorcerer of the Court.

Tantalon—a wise man whose loyalty to Gallantaria was beyond question, a man whose devotions to the mystic arts placed him above their own mundane political ambitions. Tantalon was a prime candidate. The matter was quickly agreed.

As it turned out, the ageing sorcerer was a fine choice. A brilliant strategist, his battle plans altered the whole course of the war. Two years later, Gallantaria's power had been established. The other three kingdoms were ready for truce. But the war had proved a great strain for Tantalon. His strength was fading. The Treaty of Peace, though formally signed, would last no more than a year. Neighbouring Brice was an unruly kingdom and would not hold to its terms of peace for long.

Tantalon realized that his successor must be found, and quickly, before the scheming Inner Council usurped the throne.

This was one problem, but there were many others. During the war, affairs of the homeland had been neglected. And many affairs needed attention—too many for an old man. Tantalon was deep in thought. Which were the most pressing?

Undoubtedly, recovery of the Crystal of Supremity was imperative. Pilfered in the Ham on its way to Lendle, the regency jewel had fallen into the hands of the wicked man-bull when the plundering thieves unwittingly chose the Minotaur's labyrinth as a hiding place. This heirloom of Gallantaria's regency must be returned to court.

Winter was coming and the kingdom must eat. The Netherworld sorcerers had cursed the coast with a ferocious demon fish, which tore apart fishing vessels and could eat a man whole. Since that day no fisherman would dare put to sea. Should he sail to the fishing ports to seek out the monster? But then the grain harvest had been poor and, unless the Eedetide could be tamed, the cropland would again be flooded, ruining the next autumn's harvest. Perhaps he ought to ride downstream to check the dam's progress. Or perhaps grain could be bought from neighbouring Ruddlestone. But the war effort had severely depleted his treasury. Could he raise taxes? Not a good idea, as this would mean starvation for many of the peasants. But gold reserves were low and .... *gold reserves*?

His anger rose at the thought of that unpunished scavenger beast lurking in the Cragrocks. *The Brimstone Dragon*, plundering hard-earned wealth from the Whitewater Valley. But none would venture to the Cragrock foothills to match the creature, none of sound mind at least—except perhaps the mighty Hornhelm, champion of Forrin. But Tantalon was forgetting. Hornhelm was no more. His bravery at the Battle of Skynn had won

Gallantaria the day but cost the man of bronze his life. A posthumous knighthood must be awarded to honour him and his widow. Hornhelm had been a fearless warrior, bowing neither to beast nor magic-user. How Tantalon wished he was still at court.

The sorcerer's thoughts turned to his other nobles. There was little hope for Sir Duke the Merciful, whose good nature had led him into a simple trap. Sent east to defend the Witchtooth Line, his own troops had borne witness as he turned to stone before the cunning Medusa posing as a beggar woman. As he stepped up to drop a coin into her cup, her shroud fell back to reveal that hideous serpent-haired head.

And bold Sir Dunstable, en route up the Border River, captured by river pirates and held captive at Stinn Castle. Most certainly a rescue expedition must be despatched straightaway to free the knight. Then there was Tag.

Tantalon's teeth ground tightly at the thought. Yes, 'King' Tag must be dragged from his rathole, wherever he was. Even two years of war had not wiped the memory of Tag's treachery at Narrow Pass from Tantalon's mind. The traitor must be brought to justice. Fagorn, the blind seer, or perhaps the Four Princes may know of Tag's whereabouts; they were all from the north kingdom. But no. The Ham Princes were being held by the night priests. Another expedition must be organized.

Would this curse of evil ever be wiped from the land? That verminpit at Weirtown must be first for the scourge. Tantalon sighed. So many things to do, so many things to do ...

These thoughts and more tormented the wizard as he rested after the signing ceremony. Eventually, Tantalon raised himself from his throne. He had decided what to do.

Three days later, horsemen were despatched to the four corners of the kingdom announcing a challenge. Adventurers and fortune-hunters from far and wide began to arrive at the castle gates of Royal Lendle.

Tantalon had decided that the court needed new blood, new ideas, new faces—a new breath of life. To search out the wisest, most intelligent and courageous minds in the kingdom he had designed a grand adventure quest which would test the abilities of all those who entered to their limits. No one, he thought, would be capable of fulfilling all these labours. But at the back of his mind there was a spark of hope....

As the many hundreds of contestants made their ways to take up the challenge at Royal Lendle, YOU arrived at the wizard's court. Gaining audience with Tantalon himself, you receive your instructions on a scroll of parchment. The scroll describes twelve challenging tasks, each a trial of wisdom and ingenuity and each with one common theme: *the solution to each task is a number!* The winning contestant must add up the twelve numbers (one for each task) and return to court with the correct total – this final number can only be discovered if all twelve tasks have been successfully completed. With this final answer the contestant may claim the reward of Tantalon.

Can you succeed in Gallantaria's greatest contest? Have you the valour, the wisdom and the determination to succeed in an adventure quest which became known as .....

THE TASKS OF TANTALON

Release Sir Dunstable of Aiken
Four moons ago as captive taken

THE port at Eedefork bustled with activity as merchants, fishermen and seafarers went about their business. You quickly located a vessel which would take you up the Border River. It was a cargo ship—Captain Schankerman at the helm.

'Sir Dunstable, eh?' said Schankerman as you explained the purpose of your trip. 'Yes, I knew the man. And a fine gentleman he was. He and Sir Clance of Cygnet were set upon by river pirates as they sailed up the Border. Old Dunstable was given up as dead, but a fat merchant from Thax told me he'd been captured and slung into the dungeons at Stinn Castle.'

Eventually the fort at Stinn came into view. Schankerman pointed it out. His voice dropped to a whisper, 'See that tall oak just in front of the castle? Just by its trunk you'll find an opening which leads right into the dungeons. Take care. *And Good Luck to you.*'

He did not lie. A trap door hidden in the grass by the tall tree opened the way to the bowels of the castle. You followed the narrow passage to its end. You now stand in a dimly-lit corridor in the Stinn dungeon. Cautiously searching the dungeon, you open a door into a torture room from which a low moaning is coming. You stifle a gasp as you recognize the emaciated figure of Sir Dunstable! He is suspended over a flaming pit by a rope connected to a lever by a complex series of pulleys. You step up to the lever and consider the mechanisms. You will raise him from the pit if you move the lever in the correct direction, but if you choose the wrong position, you will seal the fate of the noble knight.

Can you rescue the good knight?

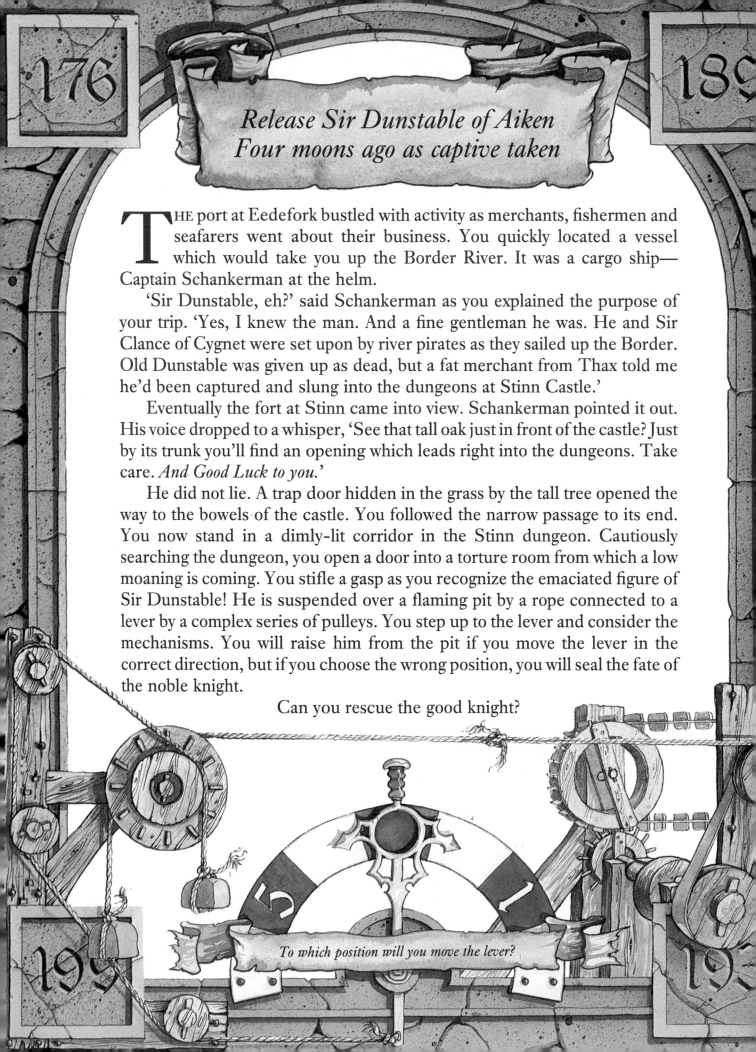

To which position will you move the lever?

The Demon Fish must terrorize
No more the shores of Fickling Rise

THE second stage of your quest takes you to Fickling, a fortified town at the mouth of the Eede. A tall castle, high on the Rise, overlooks the sea. Just down from the castle on the sea shore is a small fishing village where a spirit of gloom hangs in the air. You eat that night at an inn, sitting at a table with the local fishermen. Their eyes widen as you explain your arrival.

Their laughter mocks you. A fisherman shouts out: 'And they tell us that Tantalon is a wise man! *Ha!* First of all he sends that young whippersnapper Sir Beade for supervision of the verminpit, then he sends us *you* to rid us of the Demon Fish. Why, the fellow is surely age-crazed!'

'Be not a fool, stranger,' adds a gruff-voiced old man puffing on a long clay pipe. 'No fisherman alive can take that monster. And none of sound mind will be foolhardy enough to try!'

Later, as you lie in your bed, you consider how best to tackle the great beast. First of all you must find out what you can about the creature—where it swims and what it eats. You spend the next morning learning of the habits of the sea creatures. Then, before you can begin to fish for the Demon Fish, you must buy your bait.

What bait will you buy to help you fish for the Demon Fish? Minnows will cost you three Copper Pieces; worms will cost two Copper Pieces. Flies or meat will be more expensive, at six and seven Copper Pieces respectively.

Choose your bait carefully. How many Copper Pieces will you spend?

The Hag-Witch of Weirtown runs free
Arrest this foe—Bring her to me

THAT night, the festivities at Fickling are in your honour. The villagers are anxious to show their gratitude. The apothecary presents you with a special gift. He hands you a small vial of liquid.

'This potion,' he announces, 'is my greatest achievement. Drink this and, for a short while, you may walk unseen. I know you must face one of the fire-breathers. With this you will be safe.'

The next morning, your journey continues, following the River Weir to Weirtown, verminpit of the kingdom. Unsavoury creatures from throughout Gallantaria have been drawn to Weirtown and its dark ways.

The Hag-Witch is a sorceress of great skill who is a constant nuisance to Gallantaria's white magicians. You plan to surprise and subdue her before she can use her powers. Creeping up to her dwelling, you peep through the window. She is asleep in a chair! You heave at the door and charge into the room. In an instant, the sleeping figure has disappeared! A chuckle behind makes you spin round ...

The Hag-Witch, cackling slyly, is hobbling down the steps from the door into the street. You have been tricked! But this old, hobbling woman is no match for your speed. You spring forwards. But just as quickly you stop dead in your tracks, unable to believe your eyes.

Two identical witches are running on ahead. Seconds later *another* double has appeared and all three turn the corner into the market square! You compose yourself and follow. But as you enter the market square, your hope dies. The cunning hag has continued the illusion and now a number of likenesses have spread around the market. How will you catch her now?
Your only chance is to pursue and capture
each image of the Hag-Witch.

How many Hag-Witches can you see?

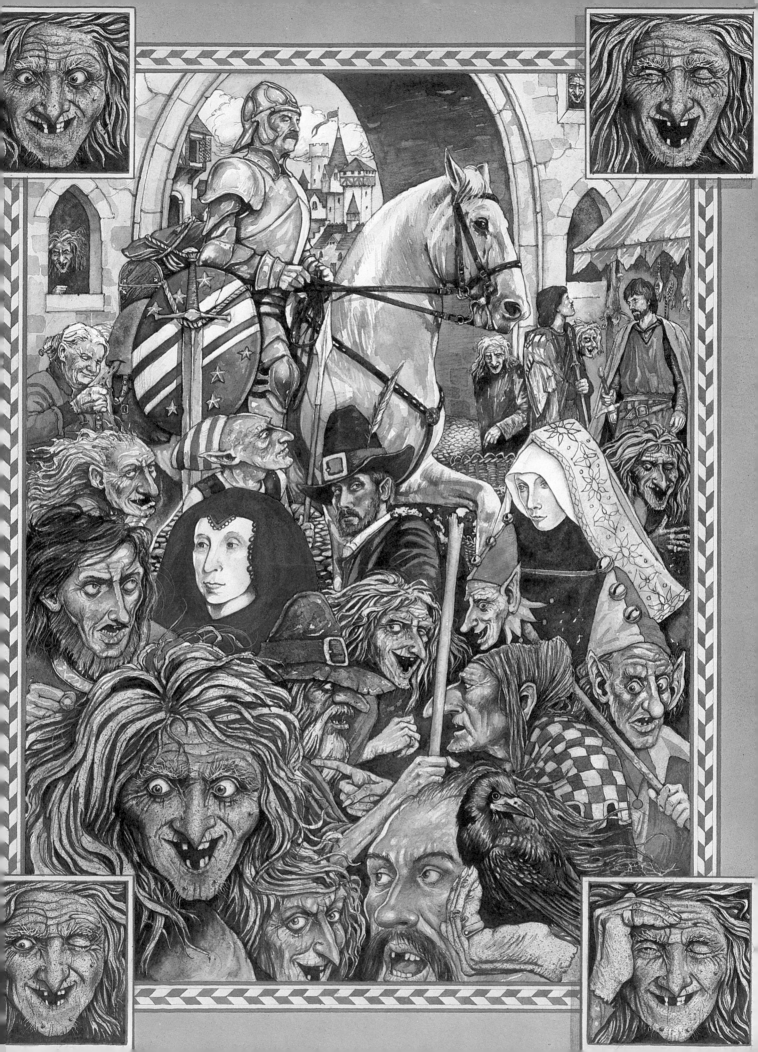

> *Four sages tried—none can succeed*
> *In holding back the River Eede*

THE various attempts to dam the Eede have all been unsuccessful. The force of the great spring floods has destroyed every barrier yet constructed. Some of the kingdom's greatest minds in engineering, agriculture and even wizardry have been set to work on preventing the annual floods which continually ruined otherwise fertile cropland. All have failed to stem the flow of the great river.

When you arrive at the site of the newly-constructed dam, a heated argument is taking place between a group of elderly scholars. You join them to see whether you can be of help.

The theory is sound. Rather than cutting off entirely the river's flow, their dam is designed to *control* it. Water flows from the river into a complex series of pipes through eight tap valves. Thus more, or less, water will flow according to how the taps are set. But, alas, the scholars have lost their master plan! Without dismantling the dam they cannot know how their taps are set and thus they may not control the river's flow.

Studying the present flow of the water, you are able to deduce that only three of the valves must be turned off to stop the flow entirely.

Which valves will you close?

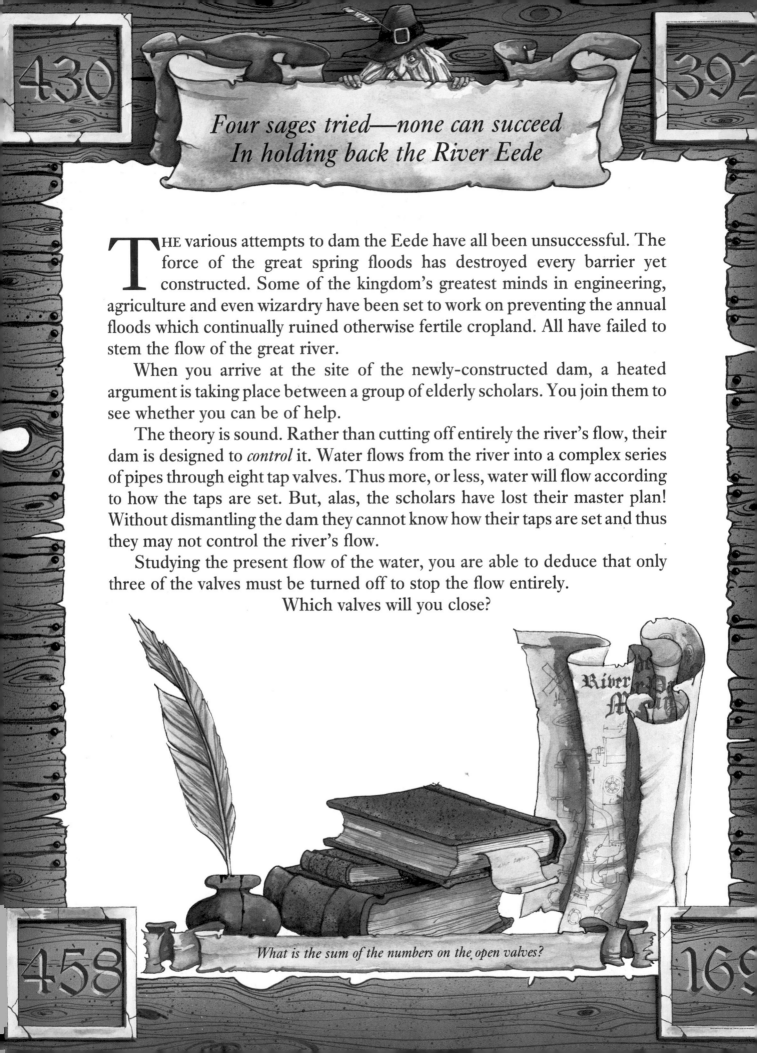

What is the sum of the numbers on the open valves?

The Brimstone Dragon foe of old
Bring home to court its hoard of gold

THE southern reaches of the Cragrock Peak foothills are avoided by all but the most foolhardy of Gallantaria. Great beasts—behemoths of a bygone age—have migrated to the Cragrocks over the centuries and now a precarious territorial balance exists.

The town of Klisdon is the last outpost of civilization before the Dark Cliffs. At the *Pig and Goblet* you meet Chauncey, a sprightly dwarf, fond of his ale. The men of Klisdon are well known for their miserliness and Chauncey is no exception; the drinking is all at your expense.

But his stories and his knowledge of the area are well worth a few mugs of ale. He has met many of the kingdom's nobles: Sir Tag of Casper and his ailing wife Davina; Sir Duke and his identical twin brother Sir Beade; even the noble Sir Dunstable and his half-cousin Sir Clance. Chauncey has met them all. He is happy to describe the route northwards.

Following his directions the next day, you reach the lair of the Brimstone Dragon in late afternoon. A gaping cave entrance is set in the towering Cragrock hillside. The cave is shallow, but its proportions are enormous. A deep snorting from inside confirms your suspicions. The beast is at home!

A first sighting of the creature makes your heart leap. Atop a rich pile of gold, silver, gems and jewels, the Dragon sits on its hoard. But you have with you the vial presented by the apothecary of Fickling. You swallow the potion.

Cautiously, you step forwards into the Dragon's cave.
The potion works! The beast cannot see you!
Whilst you remain invisible, you may
now collect its treasure.

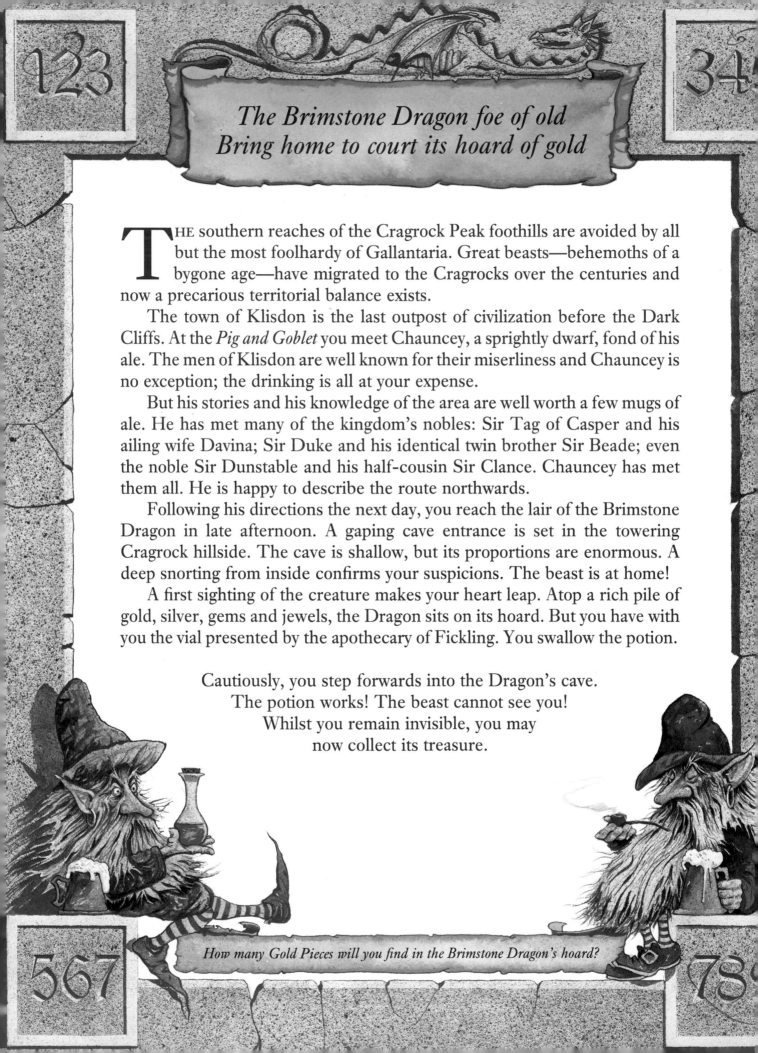

How many Gold Pieces will you find in the Brimstone Dragon's hoard?

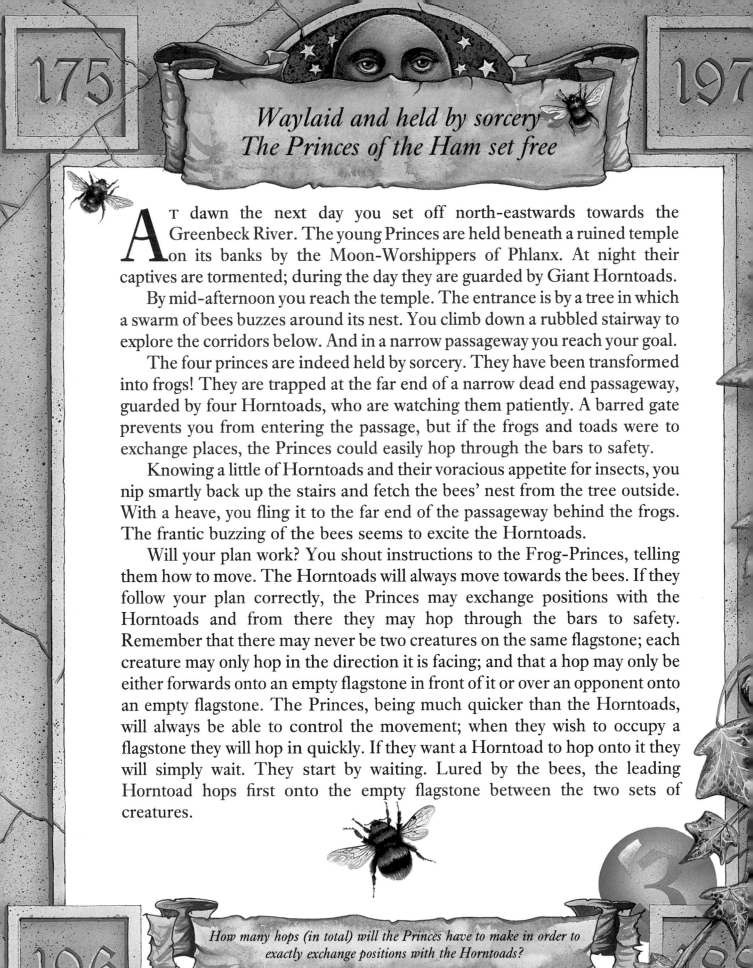

Waylaid and held by sorcery
The Princes of the Ham set free

Aᴛ dawn the next day you set off north-eastwards towards the Greenbeck River. The young Princes are held beneath a ruined temple on its banks by the Moon-Worshippers of Phlanx. At night their captives are tormented; during the day they are guarded by Giant Horntoads.

By mid-afternoon you reach the temple. The entrance is by a tree in which a swarm of bees buzzes around its nest. You climb down a rubbled stairway to explore the corridors below. And in a narrow passageway you reach your goal.

The four princes are indeed held by sorcery. They have been transformed into frogs! They are trapped at the far end of a narrow dead end passageway, guarded by four Horntoads, who are watching them patiently. A barred gate prevents you from entering the passage, but if the frogs and toads were to exchange places, the Princes could easily hop through the bars to safety.

Knowing a little of Horntoads and their voracious appetite for insects, you nip smartly back up the stairs and fetch the bees' nest from the tree outside. With a heave, you fling it to the far end of the passageway behind the frogs. The frantic buzzing of the bees seems to excite the Horntoads.

Will your plan work? You shout instructions to the Frog-Princes, telling them how to move. The Horntoads will always move towards the bees. If they follow your plan correctly, the Princes may exchange positions with the Horntoads and from there they may hop through the bars to safety. Remember that there may never be two creatures on the same flagstone; each creature may only hop in the direction it is facing; and that a hop may only be either forwards onto an empty flagstone in front of it or over an opponent onto an empty flagstone. The Princes, being much quicker than the Horntoads, will always be able to control the movement; when they wish to occupy a flagstone they will hop in quickly. If they want a Horntoad to hop onto it they will simply wait. They start by waiting. Lured by the bees, the leading Horntoad hops first onto the empty flagstone between the two sets of creatures.

How many hops (in total) will the Princes have to make in order to exactly exchange positions with the Horntoads?

The regent's jewel must no more
Be wielded by the Minotaur

As you climb the stairs into the daylight above, with the four small frogs cradled in your hands, a transformation takes place. The sun's rays fall upon the creatures and they slowly change shape to become once more four fine young men. The Princes are more than grateful for their rescue and wish to help you in return.

'My brothers and I do not envy you this task,' warns Prince Hanna. 'Indeed we know of the man-bull. The creature dwells in an underground maze by the widest point of the Eede.'

The youngest Prince whispers to Hanna, who nods in agreement. 'My little brother suggests you seek out Fagorn, the seer. Though his eyes see no more, his mind has far greater powers of sight. Follow the Eede towards its mouth and you will find Fagorn's home. Mention the name of Hanna, Prince of Chessog. Perhaps Fagorn may aid you.' You thank the Princes and set off.

Eventually you find the old man's hovel. At the mention of Prince Hanna's name, he bids you welcome and invites you in for the night. The blind man listens attentively as you relate your exploits. 'You are indeed a courageous adventurer!' laughs Fagorn. 'But you will need all your courage and more to face the man-bull and recover the regency jewel. Four paths lead into his maze. But only one path is unguarded. The others are all lain with deadly traps. If you choose the correct path you will be able to surprise the creature and defeat him. I know not which is the safe route but can tell you this. The Orb of Shantos, fashioned in blue crystal, knows the secret of the Minotaur's passages. Its advice will lead you safely to the creature.'

As you leave the next morning, Fagorn hands you a parchment scroll. 'Take this with you,' he says, 'and study it. For it is a map of the Minotaur's labyrinth. Study it well. Also, I know your journey will take you to Casper. The object of your search has been stolen by Morphus. Seek this man out.'

Some time later you reach the cave leading to the man-bull's domain. You pause to study your map. Which of the four entrances will you choose?

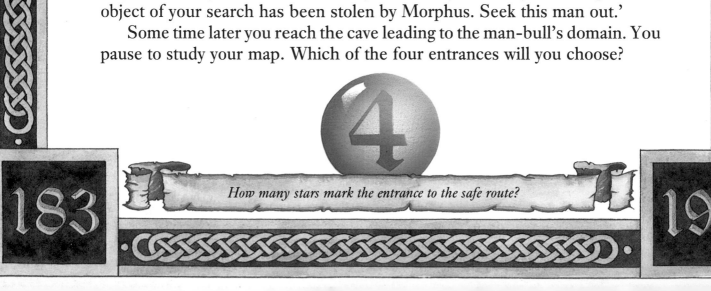

How many stars mark the entrance to the safe route?

Seek out the Ting Ring but be wise
It has the power to disguise

You emerge from the labyrinth and set off immediately for Casper, for your next task is to find the Ting Ring.

The Ting Ring was forged by the Netherworld Sorcerers, an ancient race living high in the Cragrocks. Their finest achievement, the Ting Ring, was stolen many years ago by Zarl, a necromancer from Casper. Such power is bestowed upon its owner that Gallantaria will be safe only if the Ring is presented to the custody of the court at Lendle. On Zarl's death, the ring never reappeared. But this was hardly surprising in view of one of its special powers. For the Ting Ring had the chameleon-like power to blend in with its surroundings, making it nigh on impossible to locate.

Following Fagorn's advice, you begin your search with the laboratories of Morphus the alchemist, to whom all of Zarl's possessions were bequeathed on his death. But finding the ageing alchemist is no easy task. The folk of Casper seem to hold a fear of the powers of Morphus and none are willing to direct you to his laboratory. Eventually you learn of its whereabouts from a miserable rat-catcher named Chagg, but at a cost of a couple of copper pieces.

Morphus, of course, denies all knowledge of the ring. He believes the Ting Ring to have been lost altogether when Zarl died. But does he lie?

Can you locate the Ting Ring?

If you are able to find the Ting Ring, you will be able to answer this question:
How many stones are set in the ring?

In exile living underground
King Tag of Casper must be found

EVER since the episode at Narrow Pass, Tag had earned the name of 'The Betrayer'. Having made a somewhat unholy alliance with the regent of Brice, Tag had laid plans for the murder of his own King Constain. During the second year of the war he had arranged the infamous ambush in Narrow Pass. On that fateful day Tag himself was escorting the King, riding with his queen back towards Forrin from the North Kingdom. When they reached Narrow Pass, a party of rebellious Northlanders isolated the royal party and all were slain. It was Tag himself who dealt the death blow to Constain.

A self-proclaimed king, his traitorous act was exposed, forcing him to flee to the countryside. Rumour has it that he is now hiding between Casper and the Greenbeck.

You set off on Tag's trail. Travelling across from Casper towards Chessog you can only pick up meagre clues to his whereabouts.

On fleeing from Casper, King Tag met the Lady Davina, his Queen, at a secret rendezvous point due north in the shadow of Mount Cuspid. Together they rode southwards through the night to Eacham Abbey to meet their friend and spiritual guide, the Bishop of Eacham. A faithful ally, the Bishop escorted them three days later to Greycloud Manor, home of Sir Neibling, Knight of Eacham. But even this friend was forced to turn them out when, two nights later, a band of loyalist vigilantes were scouted to the north.

But here your trail has ended. Where is King Tag likely to be now? The traitor's hiding place is shown on the map.

If you can deduce where King Tag is hiding, read off the north-south and east-west co-ordinates of his refuge and add them together.

The Golden Cross from Hornhelm's Crown
Must be returned to Forrin Town

YOUR next task takes you south-westwards again to Forrin Town for another hunt, this time for the treasure of Hornhelm. A gallant commander in the war, Hornhelm has already become a legend with the people of Forrin. His acts of courage will be remembered with pride through the ages. But, alas, noble Hornhelm was struck down in battle.

Fearing an invasion, Hornhelm had taken steps to guard his personal riches, plundered from the enemy. His treasure, and the fabled Golden Cross, had been secretly buried for safekeeping. But his death was untimely. He alone knew of the treasure's whereabouts.

You return to Forrin and gain audience with Serendra, Hornhelm's lady. Taking you into her trust, she gives you the only clue to Hornhelm's secret—a scroll which bears a map and a message.

At sunrise the next morning you arrive on Windswept Moor. Can you locate Hornhelm's treasure?

FROM THE TALLEST TREE ON WINDSWEPT MOOR, WALK TOWARDS THE NEAREST PATH. FOLLOW IT TO THE RIGHT UNTIL YOU REACH A BRIDGE WALK UPSTREAM UNTIL TWO BUILDINGS ARE DIRECTLY IN LINE. THEN TURN EASTWARDS AND CONTINUE UNTIL YOU REACH A PATH. HALFWAY BETWEEN THIS POINT AND THE NEAREST BUILDING, DIG UNDER A BU

If you can locate the treasure, you will be able to answer this question:
How many trees grow next to the tallest tree on Windswept Moor?

THE SPIRIT OF HORNHELM
WILL HAUNT FOREVER THOSE WHO DIG FOR SELFISH GAIN. WHATEVER
IS TO BE FOUND BELONGS RIGHTFULLY TO THE PEOPLE OF FORRIN

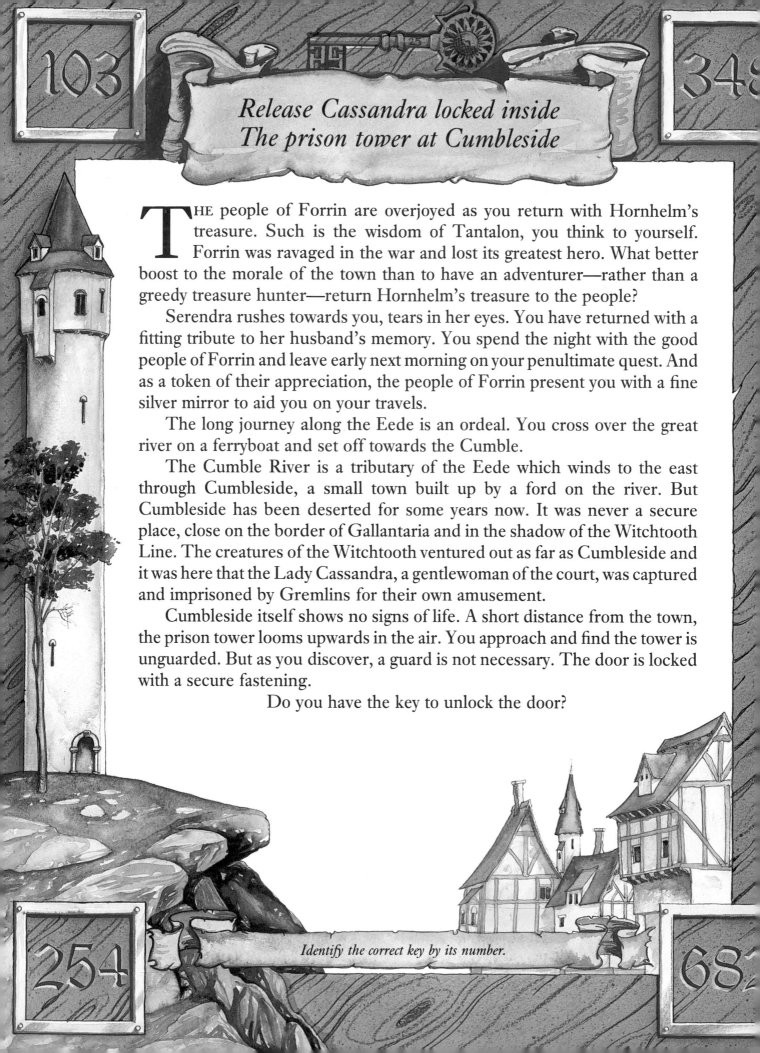

Release Cassandra locked inside
The prison tower at Cumbleside

THE people of Forrin are overjoyed as you return with Hornhelm's treasure. Such is the wisdom of Tantalon, you think to yourself. Forrin was ravaged in the war and lost its greatest hero. What better boost to the morale of the town than to have an adventurer—rather than a greedy treasure hunter—return Hornhelm's treasure to the people?

Serendra rushes towards you, tears in her eyes. You have returned with a fitting tribute to her husband's memory. You spend the night with the good people of Forrin and leave early next morning on your penultimate quest. And as a token of their appreciation, the people of Forrin present you with a fine silver mirror to aid you on your travels.

The long journey along the Eede is an ordeal. You cross over the great river on a ferryboat and set off towards the Cumble.

The Cumble River is a tributary of the Eede which winds to the east through Cumbleside, a small town built up by a ford on the river. But Cumbleside has been deserted for some years now. It was never a secure place, close on the border of Gallantaria and in the shadow of the Witchtooth Line. The creatures of the Witchtooth ventured out as far as Cumbleside and it was here that the Lady Cassandra, a gentlewoman of the court, was captured and imprisoned by Gremlins for their own amusement.

Cumbleside itself shows no signs of life. A short distance from the town, the prison tower looms upwards in the air. You approach and find the tower is unguarded. But as you discover, a guard is not necessary. The door is locked with a secure fastening.

Do you have the key to unlock the door?

Identify the correct key by its number.

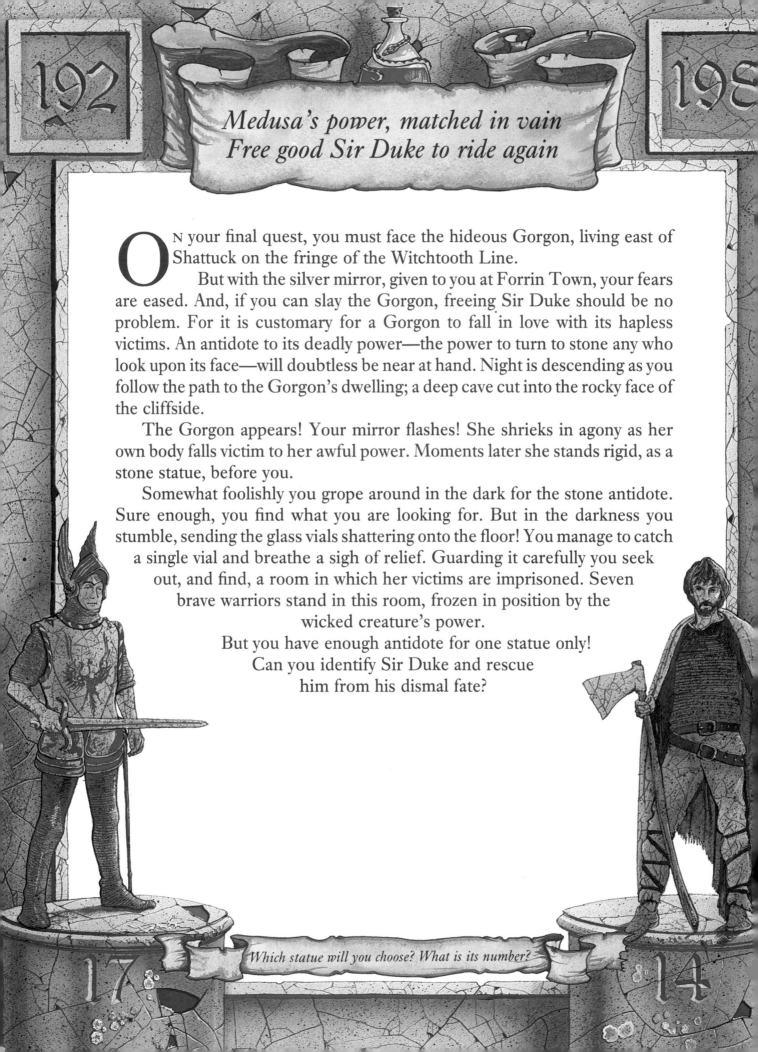

Medusa's power, matched in vain
Free good Sir Duke to ride again

ON your final quest, you must face the hideous Gorgon, living east of Shattuck on the fringe of the Witchtooth Line.

But with the silver mirror, given to you at Forrin Town, your fears are eased. And, if you can slay the Gorgon, freeing Sir Duke should be no problem. For it is customary for a Gorgon to fall in love with its hapless victims. An antidote to its deadly power—the power to turn to stone any who look upon its face—will doubtless be near at hand. Night is descending as you follow the path to the Gorgon's dwelling; a deep cave cut into the rocky face of the cliffside.

The Gorgon appears! Your mirror flashes! She shrieks in agony as her own body falls victim to her awful power. Moments later she stands rigid, as a stone statue, before you.

Somewhat foolishly you grope around in the dark for the stone antidote. Sure enough, you find what you are looking for. But in the darkness you stumble, sending the glass vials shattering onto the floor! You manage to catch a single vial and breathe a sigh of relief. Guarding it carefully you seek out, and find, a room in which her victims are imprisoned. Seven brave warriors stand in this room, frozen in position by the wicked creature's power.

But you have enough antidote for one statue only!
Can you identify Sir Duke and rescue
him from his dismal fate?

Which statue will you choose? What is its number?

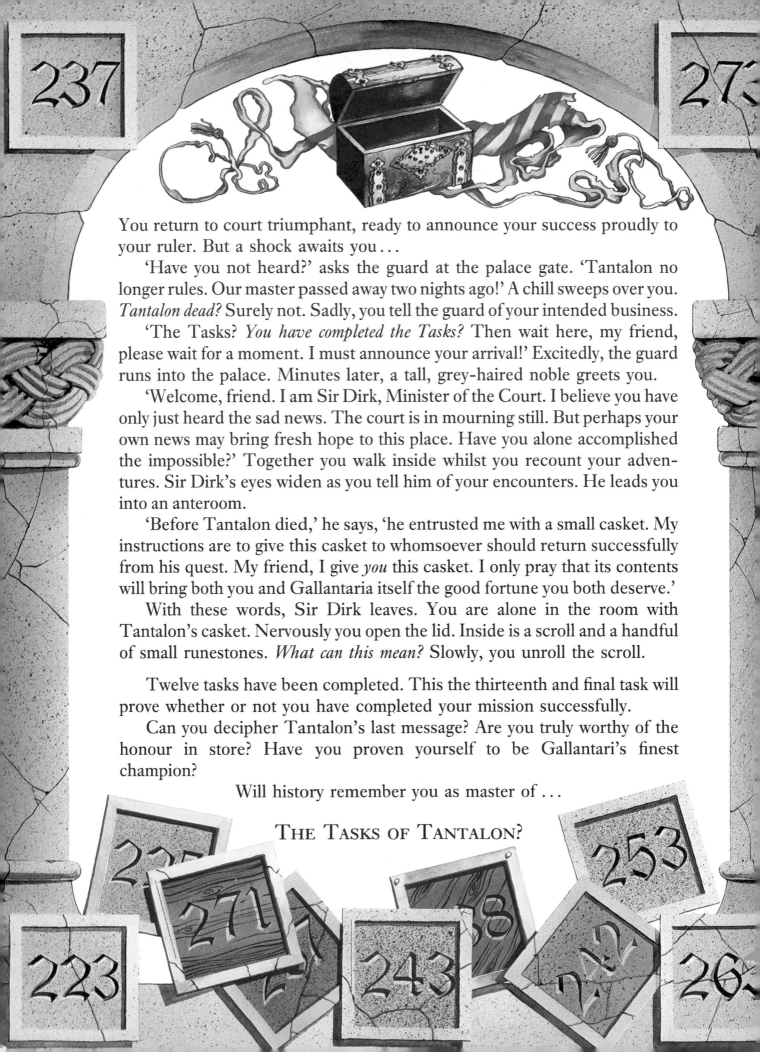

237 273

You return to court triumphant, ready to announce your success proudly to your ruler. But a shock awaits you...

'Have you not heard?' asks the guard at the palace gate. 'Tantalon no longer rules. Our master passed away two nights ago!' A chill sweeps over you. *Tantalon dead?* Surely not. Sadly, you tell the guard of your intended business.

'The Tasks? *You have completed the Tasks?* Then wait here, my friend, please wait for a moment. I must announce your arrival!' Excitedly, the guard runs into the palace. Minutes later, a tall, grey-haired noble greets you.

'Welcome, friend. I am Sir Dirk, Minister of the Court. I believe you have only just heard the sad news. The court is in mourning still. But perhaps your own news may bring fresh hope to this place. Have you alone accomplished the impossible?' Together you walk inside whilst you recount your adventures. Sir Dirk's eyes widen as you tell him of your encounters. He leads you into an anteroom.

'Before Tantalon died,' he says, 'he entrusted me with a small casket. My instructions are to give this casket to whomsoever should return successfully from his quest. My friend, I give *you* this casket. I only pray that its contents will bring both you and Gallantaria itself the good fortune you both deserve.'

With these words, Sir Dirk leaves. You are alone in the room with Tantalon's casket. Nervously you open the lid. Inside is a scroll and a handful of small runestones. *What can this mean?* Slowly, you unroll the scroll.

Twelve tasks have been completed. This the thirteenth and final task will prove whether or not you have completed your mission successfully.

Can you decipher Tantalon's last message? Are you truly worthy of the honour in store? Have you proven yourself to be Gallantari's finest champion?

Will history remember you as master of ...

THE TASKS OF TANTALON?

237 271 8 253 223 243 26

"I TANTALON, HAVE LEFT THIS LIFE
MY WAR-TORN KINGDOM CURSED WITH STRIFE
ONE HOPE REMAINS, A CHAMPION BOLD
WILL RID THE TROUBLES TAKING HOLD
YOUR TASKS ARE DONE BUT ONE MORE QUEST
REMAINS TO PROVE YOU TRULY BEST
THE ANSWERS TO THE TASKS YOU'VE DONE
HAVE ALL BEEN NUMBERS; IF THEY'RE SUMMED
THE STARTING POINT YOU THEN WILL FIND
AND THROUGH A RUNESEARCH YOU MUST WIND
SO SEARCH YOUR RUNE WITH OPEN EYES
AND OPEN MIND, IF YOU BE WISE
BUT IF YOUR TASKS BE INCORRECT
THEIR SUM, IN ERROR, WILL REFLECT
THIS FACT, AS YOU WILL FIND NO STONE
AND THUS SHALL STAY THE TRUTH UNKNOWN
A HUNTER WITH NO BOW MAY HELP
THIS TASK TOO TRYING FOR A WHELP
MARK NOT HIS WORD AS IT APPEARS
INSTEAD SEEK WHAT WILL FADE WITH YEARS

IF YOU FIND THE RUNETRAIL TRUE
THEN YOUR REWARD IS OVERDUE
FOR IF YOU SOLVE THIS LAST RUNESEARCH
YOUR HONOUR IS THE HIGHEST PERCH."

TANTALON OF GALLANTARIA.

251 274 272 256 267

PRETENDERS AND FOOLS WILL END THEIR QUESTS HERE.
ONLY A TRUE CHAMPION WILL REACH THE ULTIMATE GOAL